NORTH WINTER

By Hayden Carruth

Decorations by Dale Ballantyne

The Prairie Press

IOWA CITY

✳

*Although first accepted for book publication by The Prairie Press,
an earlier draft of this poem was published in the Virginia
Quarterly Review, and was awarded a prize in the Emily Clark
Balch competition for 1964, sponsored by the University of
Virginia. The author extends acknowledgment and
thanks to all concerned.*

FOR ROSE MARIE

NORTH WINTER

❄

I

Coming of winter
is a beech sapling
rising silverly
in a brown field
in bramble in
thicket the raspberry
the rosemallow
all gone to rust
a silver sapling
to which in wind
and the judaskisses
of snow the starved
brown leaves cling
and cling.

2

In spring the mountain was a fish
   with blond scales
in summer the mountain was a crab
   with a green shell
in fall the mountain was a leopard
   with a burnished coat
in winter the mountain is a bird
   with lavender feathers
   and a still heart.

3

Snow

      ice

            bitter wind

     the body of love.

4

Where two boots labored yesterday across the
    snowdrifted pasture
today each boothole is an offertory of
    bright seeds
bittersweet yellowbirch hemlock pine thistle
    burning unconsumed.

5

   Stronger than destiny is pain
   and in the leaf
   the marvelous venature is stronger
   and in the year
   the last morsel of pancake
   of the forty-third breakfast
   is stronger.

6

Caught in a brier of stars
the lunar scrap

         blurred
like paper flickering in a gale
carrying away a scarcely remembered
poem of a summer night.

7

Twenty-two degrees below zero
and only the blade of meadow
like a snowpetal or foil of platinum
to defend the house against the glistening
mountain and the near unwinking
moon.

8

The morning ice on the window
is opaque as beaten silver
and the poet in his ninefootsquare hut
stamps rhythmically breathing out plume
after plume of warmth while the stove
nibbles a few frozen sticks.

9

In the snowy woods of morning
the new deer tracks run
cross and criss and circle among
the snowapparelled spruces and the
gray maples telling of revels by night
of joy and delight and happiness
beyond any power of consciousness
although the small green pellets
mean a hard diet.

10

The tamarack with needles lost
and a thousand curled stiff twigs
like dead birdsfeet takes
the snow greedily and in snatches
to cover its misshapen nakedness.

11

A winter's tale is told in
rumors of snow
sneaping winds
the frazil flux of identities
tardy recognitions
the living stones.

12

Think not of chaste snow always
nor of crystalline coldness think
of spruce boughs like the swordblade
breasts of negresses and of the bull
mountain humped over the white soft
valley and of stags raging down
the rutting wind and of northern
passion crackling like naked trumpets
in the snow under the blazing aurora.

13

The song of the gray
ninepointed buck
contains much contains
many contains all
a whole north for
example the sweet
sharp whistling of
the redpolls caught
overhead in the branches
of the yellow birch
like leaves left over
from autumn and at
night the remote
chiming of stars
caught in the tines
of his quiet exaltation.

14

The arctic owl moved across the snowsmooth
meadow to the dark balsam without sound
without wingbeat more quiet than a fish
more effortless than the gliding seed
as if it were a white thought of love
moving moving over the pasture to home.

15

Five
jays
discuss
goodandevil
in a
white
birch
like five
blue
fingers
playing
a
guitar.

16

Eons gone by the sea
hissed among these promontories
in ageless stress and despair
now stilled
but memorialized
in the frozen whirl and floodtide of the snow.

17

Like a frozen lake the sky on the bitterest
night cracks in rays a black elm
rising a spray of limbs revealing
the longdrowned lurid moon.

18

The frozen
brook sprawls
in sunlight
a tree of glass
uprooted.

19

Cold hunger tripped her but her years
held her downfallen in this snow hollow
this small death valley where small beaks
and talons will slowly chip her frozen
being though in the snow desert she will
not bleach and her eyes will stay soft
and beautiful a long long time in the
winter light and she will modestly wear
her genteel tatters of old flesh and fur.

20

Snow buntings whirling
on a snowy field
cutglass reflections
on a ceiling.

21

The dog flies with his ears
across the snow carrying a
deer's legbone in his jaws
the bone flops threejointedly
and the little hoof dances
delicately in the snow.

22

The window
      the icicle
           the gleaming moon
when the lamplight fails.

23

The night is an immense cauldron
four farms of boiling snow under
a gale from the pole and the highway
where headlights cringe
seethes with a furious froth
and melts away.

24

This wind this
screaming parrot
this springing
wolf this down
fall this ab
solute extinc
tion this deton
ating godhead
this wind this.

25

Blizzard trampling past has left
the birches bent as in humiliation
the soft scotch pines laid down
as in subjection the beeches snapped
at the top as in a reign of terror
the balsams scarred but upright
as in the dignity of suffering and all
the woods in sorrow as if the world
meant something.

26

Pale dawnlight spooks the mist
and the valley glimmers and
higher behind the mountain
whitely rises a farther peak
in remote majesty a presence
silent and unknown and gone
by noon.

27

Harlequin
is said to assimilate himself to a condition
of animal grace

let him study
the fore hoof of the pinto searching for grass
in the snowy pasture.

28

In cold
      the snow
leaps and
         dances
lightly
      over the
earth
     but in thaw
the sullen fingers
of snow heavily
cling to each stalk
and to every stone.

29

Tracks of the snowshoe rabbit across the
snow
are a ridiculous ominous alphabet of
skulls.

30

The brook has holes in its cover
this morning
where the black water flows
rippling menacing
under the snow

which mounds in untouched purity
except where
threaded prints of the mink
delicately deathly
stop to drink.

31

Snow comes
bits of light
flake from the sky
day breaks
whirling
in early night.

32

Beginning with the palest and softest lavender

deepening

downward

murex

purpure

arras of

old brocade

kingly

loveliest hues

imaginable

snow blending

the naked

hardwood

maples

beeches

birches

forests called

green in summer

now this

unbelievable

intricacy

shaded

purple

gray

hanging

wavering

trembling

over the

valley

this is our wintering mountain.

33

Heavy gloves
or better
      mittens
the north silencing
savoring and saving
that lewdword
finger.

34

After the thaw after
the illusion cold comes
again
     returning
changed in aspect
a great body of death
and inertia a corpse
flung down
       a whale
perhaps
     gray and still
and immense crushing
everything
      day
becomes hard and silent
night stiffens heaving
to support the weight
while the woods groan
and the soft snow
turns metallic
barren and brittle

the house creaks
under the burden in
mindless suffering
and its nails burst
out with a sound of
cracking bones
                    moon
sets in afternoon
jays huddle say
nothing and
                    endure.

35

Sky like fishblood
deprecative lurid thin
evening blush on the mountain
and here
            the foreground
very near
            a sheen
vitrescent snowcrust and
reflected light
                    thin
lurid and deprecative
                            fish
blood.

36

Gunmetal snow icecolored sky
granitic meadow sullen noon
stunted yellowed loplimbed pine
flayed birch elm decorated
with empty nests poverty
hunger red fingers retracting
in splayed gloves dead sun
gray hair poverty poverty.

37

Wet fire
it turns out
is better than
no
fire.

38

Sky yellow sky
wet sky reeky
sky lax some
god's old diaper.

39

When some amazonian indians for whom
all experience had been degrees of heat
were given a hunk of ice to touch they said
it's hot
      the eskimo child that tumbled
on the other hand into the fire did not
say it was cold
          nevertheless
               brazil brazil
thy foolishness is also a kind of beauty.

40

The day the brook went out
was still midwinter locked
in zodiacal fastness yet
rain fell and fell in fact
so much the snow turned green
and the water in the brook
covered the ice like urine
until at one crack
the whole damned thing let go
ice and muddy water trees
stones bits of lumber snow
like a racketing express

through a local stop and then
subsided leaving the banks
dark and dirty raw and torn
with new patterns of rocks
looking unfamiliar what
a purgation it was wild
and beautiful the result
wasn't bad either all told
for now the brook is rising
again after the long
icebound repression singing
a midwinter rebel song.

41

Lover of balsam and lover of white pine
o crossbill crossbill
cracking unseen with of all things scissors
seeds seeds
a fidget for ears enpomped in the meadow's
silence silence
a crackling thorn aflame in the meadow's
cold cold.

42

Snow's downstrokes climb softly up the c   r.

                                                                  i
                    n f
          o   e

43

Lichen and liverwort
laurel and brome
lightened the gravamen
of old stones
a cellarhole far
in foliate woods
the dry cistern
where sweet water stood
the doorstone to nothing
that summer entwined
softly and now
drowned in the snow.

44

Astigmatism breaks
the crescent moon
into two images
set asymmetrically
so that they cross
in the upper third
like two scimitars
flung down at rest
on the sahara.

45

In freshfallen snow
marks of pad and paw
and even partridge claw
go delicately and distinct
straight as a string of beads
but marks of a heeled boot
waver shuffle wamble
ruckle the snow define
a most unsteady line

then spell it out once so

death knowledge being heady
it hath not the beasts' beauty
goeth tricksy and ploddy
and usually too damn wordy
but drunken or topsyturvy
gladhanding tea'd or groovy
it arriveth
it arriveth
o you pretty lady.

46

Lichen is a hardy plant
hardy hardy
         taking
sustenance from the granite ledge
nouriture from the dead elm bole
icy plant hoar plant
               living kin
to rime
       the north plant
              flower
of death poverty and resolution.

47

On Lincoln's birthday the forest
bound in fifty degrees of frost
stirs tentatively with a creaking
here and there in the new strength
of the noticeably higher sun.

48

Four greens
   the aspen trunk
   the lichen on the aspen trunk
   the shadow of the aspen across the snow
   the vanished leaves of the aspen fluttering
all over the sky.

49

Under the hill a winter twilight
darkens to evening colorlessly
without sunset and yet the birches
leaping higher across the way
cry pink cry lavender cry saffron
the instant the darkness freezes them.

50

When conditions of frost and
    moisture are just right
    the air is filled
with thousands and thousands
    of points of light
    like the fireflies come back
only tinier and much more brilliant
    as if the fireflies
    had ghosts
to haunt the february night.

51

Three
    sixteen
        seventy-nine
            five hundred
                ten thousand
                a million
                    a milliard
three

a snowsquall
                aged winter's
tantrum in the sun.

52

Small things
    are hardest to believe
a redpoll snatching
    the drops from an icicle.

Layer upon layer
        late winter snow
a dobosch torte
        compact crusts and fillings
in a cut snowbank counting
        the rings of all winter's
storms and thaws
        like a tree grown
in one season

        to which level
a boot will sink
        depends
on the resistance and
        tensility
of each stratum

        woe to him
who steps where
        the sun blared hotly
in january
        he will go in floundering go in
to his chicken neck
        woe woe.

54

In late winter cold nights and
warm days bring the untimely
harvests bright pails and smoke
in the sugarbush and the snow
called cornsnow on the mountain
whining under the skis like
scratchfeed plunging in the chute.

55

The eye of
           the hut
sheds tears
   musically

from the eye of
   the hut
glass tears fall

the tears of
   the hut
shatter and
            trickle
musically away

the hut musically
   is weeping

from the eye of
   the hut
glass tears fall and
   shatter
musically all day.

56

Where the snowbank leans
   let april waken
                let
dishevelment rise from covert
   crocus and violet rise
Persephone lift hand
   to first light
             narrowing
lashes moist of lethe
   dewpetaled diaphane
let the dogtooth
            following
   fasten in bractlet jaws
sop of the yellow blossom
   and let
            grasses rise there
unbinding anemone
   arbutus and lethargy
and the dark sward of dreams
   where the snowbank leans.

57

One day music
            begins
everywhere in the woods
unexpectedly
            water water
dripping from fir boughs
spilling from ledges

singing
            unexpectedly
as when a woman sleeping
speaks a strange word
or a name
                so winterfolk
the chickadees give over
harshness for a kind of
carol
            and the poet appears
emerges brushing the
mist from his shoulders
amused and yawning
tasting the snowwater
crumbling a bit of tanbark
in his teeth
                    water water
the pools and freshets
wakening
                earth glistening
releasing the ways of
                            the
words of
            earth long frozen.

... and sun the blear sun straggled forever
    on the horizon an unvarying scrutiny around
around as they limped and stumbled holding
    each other against the wind over the ice
that crumbled under them in the tremors of
    unseen currents and the compass plunging
and rearing the sun the livid sun smeared
    in the wind watching watching never
relenting till exhaustion inundated them
    yet they slept with their eyes open clinging
together just as they walked often with
    their eyes shut hand in hand and fell
at last tripped on their destination
    their sextant snagged their compass wild
with incomprehension and they looked
    over the sides of the world The sun
the bloated sun ever on the horizon ballooning
    and they shuddered and turned to each other
and then dropped down their plumbline
    under them and payed out its knots
hand over hand to the end to fifteen hundred
    fathoms and felt the plummet still swinging in
the void ...

      ... nothing they were nothing
    afloat on nothing frozen by the winds of
nothing under the meaningless glare of nothing's

eye there where the compass points down
there where the needle turns in . . .

                                        . . . why
        had they come so far what had led them
drawn them into the remoteness and the
        hostility of north what did north mean
and why why was one of them black and
        the other white these were the points in
doubt There in confrontation they gave over
        the last dissemblings and the last nostalgias
nothing against nothing yet more than that
        their infinitesimal nothing against the
nothing of all the nothing of the real and in
        this giddiness they became at last
the objectivists They drew back not in
        fear for fear had consumed itself
but as the painter retreats from his canvas
        and so they saved themselves now seeing
how this was the only virtue the withdrawing
        mind that steadies before reality and they
turned slowly together through the whole
        arc of absurdity with outstretched hands
bestowing cold benediction on the north
        and then sank down Another confrontation
stoned them as they peered into each other's
        eyes . . .
                        . . . and saw nothing nothing Oh
in the low gutteral inner voice they exclaimed
        the misery the destitution of nothing . . .

... and saw nothing except yes this is the
    object nothing except the other's returning
gaze which each knew also saw

                nothing

                   And
    in this likeness this scrap of likeness that
contained their likelihood they arose once
    more calmly the tall twin centers
of compassion in the wide field of cold and
    horror And the sun the huge sun circled
around them . . .

               . . . they came back trudging
    in love and hardship while the sun
took a month to set cowering lidless on the
    extremity of the ice floe where they
crouched Aurora flickered and mounted
    pale brightening caparisons of yellow
and green falling fluttering swaying
    in such majestic movements that that
elemental silence pealed with trumpets
    and they truly listened with their eyes Did
they then see with their ears the changing
    counterpoints of wind and snow the
purity of whiteness modulating everywhere
    in dunes and fastnesses and cascades
Reality gladdened them and all the more
    when the astonished walrus fell off his seat
backwards whopping the sea and they smote
    their knees and wallowed in the snow . . .

. . . north is a horror from which a horror grows
    a purity and fervor to which in opposition
an equal purity and fervor supervene north
    is the latitude of the near remote lying
beyond hope and beyond despair lying in destination
    where the compass points down the needle turns in
where the last breath of meaning is borne away
    on the cold wind north is the meaninglessness
of beauty uncaused in the complete object
    auroral flickerings on the eternal snows
the eye swimming in the mind's deluge
    the blue mountain floating on emptiness
the shadow of the white bear gliding underfoot
    north is the vacancy that flowers in a
glance wakening compassion and mercy and
    lovingkindness the beautiful dew
of the sea rosmarine the call dying in silence
    so distant so small and meeting
itself in its own silence forever north is
    north is the aurora north is
deliverance emancipation . . .

                          . . . north is

    nothing . . .

C O L O P H O N

This book has been designed by Carroll Coleman and printed at
The Prairie Press in Iowa City. The body type is Joanna,
designed by Eric Gill, and the display is Fry's eighteenth century
Old Face Open, both hand set. The paper is Curtis Rag
and the endsheets are Strathmore Artlaid.